10 × 10 + 1

More Q & A

For Sigmund Freud

By

John Griffin

Psychoanalysis is in essence a cure through love

Freud, in a letter to Jung

In loving memory of my father, Joseph J. Griffin, and my mother, Elizabeth A. (Whitehouse) Griffin, for demonstrating to me what family really means.

In loving memory of my in-laws, Richard & Joan (Crosbie) Fowler who loved family.

Preface

This is a sequel to John's first book, <u>101 Q & A For Sigmund Freud</u>. It continues in the same format as the first book with 101 questions and answers. There is blank space to write down any thoughts which may come to mind. This is not an end all or be all about Freud. I picked through many sources to bring juicy tidbits to you, the reader. Any errors fall on my shoulders and I have tried to fact check each question. Again, as I hoped in my first book, if this short tome compels you to pursue further study on Freud, then it will all have been worth it on my part.

1. Who were some of my colleagues over my lifetime?

There was Karl Abraham, Max Eitingon, Sandor Ferenczi, Ernest Jones, Otto Rank, Hanns Sachs, Wilhelm Fliess, Alfred Adler, Wilhelm Stekel, Carl Gustav Jung, Georg Groddeck, A.A. Brill, Anna Freud, and Melanie Klein.

2. Did I form a "secret society" of psychoanalysts?

Yes, I did. I am not sure how "secret" it was but it consisted of me and several of my colleagues. Yet, we tried to keep it secret. I even created a special gold ring only for members of my psychoanalytical Committee to wear.

3. When did I begin and end this "secret" inner circle?

It existed from 1912 to 1927. The initial group members were Ernest Jones, Sandor Ferenczi, Otto Rank, Hanns Sachs, Karl Abraham, Max Eitingon and myself. Due to circumstances, there seemed to be no point any longer to maintain the secrecy so the original Committee was dissolved and a new international Committee was founded.

4. What purpose did I have in mind for founding this secret committee?

It aimed at controlling psychoanalysis as a discipline and a way for me to monitor its progress. I was in charge and I let my colleagues know that. I expected allegiance to me and the Committee would be private and confidential.

5. Who was one of my star pupils you might say?

That would be Karl Abraham who I first met in 1907. Karl was the first German to practice psychoanalysis and founded the Berlin Psychoanalytical Society.

6. Some people deal well with groups, do I?

No, I don't. I am more of a solitary man. I am also not very good at running groups. Some might say that I am a bit of a loner.

7. Did I have a superstition that I would die at age 61?

Yes, I did. For a smart man, I had to work on this superstition.

8. Did I have the temperament for direct confrontation?

No, it is not in my nature to engage in that activity.

9. What physician did I first meet in 1887 with whom I would have a long ongoing correspondence with?

That would be the specialist, Ear, Nose and Throat, Dr. Wilhelm Fliess. We corresponded by letter frequently and this correspondence would eventually be book bound as they were never destroyed.

10. Was my mother's, Amalia's, heritage unique?

Yes, my mother was from the lineage of Galician Jews. She was not any ordinary Jew but came from a tough, unmannered breed with feisty mannerisms. Galician Jews actually fought against the Nazis.

11. How was my mother to live with?

She was a very spirited person and difficult to be around. She had a forceful personality.

12. As a Jew, did my mother celebrate any Jewish feasts?

No, she did not.

13. How special did my parents think I was?

I was so special that I was given a room to myself. However, one might think that I ended up a very selfish person and that was just not the case. My parents did think that I would someday be famous.

14. What did I not like throughout my entire life?

I had no like whatsoever for musical instruments. Not one of my children played an instrument.

15. Who influenced my life tremendously?

There were many but none like Jean Martin Charcot. He influenced me so much that I named my oldest son after him, Martin.

16. What did my wife and I share in common when we were first married?

We were both poor.

17. Did I ever serve in the military?

Yes, I served for one month in the Austrian army. I was commissioned as a first lieutenant and then, lastly, a captain.

18. Ironically, what did I discourage my sons from studying and entering this field?

I discouraged them from entering medicine. I believed, real or rationalized, that Jews could not make it in medicine.

19. What did I first use to get around when I opened my practice?

I would take a Fiaker, the equivalent of what you Americans might call a fancy cab. To use a single horse carriage or bus or tram would simply not be respectable for a physician. The Fiaker cost more. This put a burden on Freud as he was still poor at the beginning of his practice.

20. What quality did my wife and I raise our children to have?

We raised them to have a selfless attitude. There was no room for selfishness in our household. I can still hear my wife telling the children to divide it among yourselves.

21. How was my behavior with my children during my three month vacations?

My heart was joyous to be with my children and I believe that I acted as a good father, not lacking for attention to my children.

22. What modern device was I not very fond of using and tried to avoid so?

I did not like to use the telephone. It did not permit me to look one In the eyes to determine the truth.

23. How many hours a day did I work when I was in full practice?

I would work anywhere from sixteen to eighteen hour days.

24. What odd practice would I enjoy when I would vacation at the Adriatic?

While out far in the water, waiters would swim or wade out to bring refreshments to me and others. Sometimes they would bring cigars and matches.

25. Even though I lived in Vienna, did I like residing there?

No, it would be my choice to live elsewhere. But, as well, I could find enjoyment and I am unsure if I detested living here.

26. What was one of my most pleasurable recreational activities?

I liked taking walks and hiking with my children. We would scour for berries of all types and mushrooms and other fungi. I had a good knowledge of mushrooms to avoid any poisonous ones.

27. Did I ever do the common task of grocery shopping?

Yes, at least one time on record, I did. We were at our summer cottage and rains were washing out roads and travel paths putting our food supply in dangers. I slung on a backpack and went hiking to find food and was very successful.

28. What major piece of literature did I work on during the summer holiday of 1899 which took me away from my family?

That would be my <u>Interpretation of Dreams</u>. Sadly, it was not very well received in the professional community. It almost died so to speak.

29. What exciting event happened in 1902?

Up until that point in my life, I held an honorary title of professor. In 1902, the honor of full professor was conferred upon me.

30. What sport did I enjoy?

I liked fishing. I did not enjoy rowing.

31. Along with other talents, what did my eldest son, Martin, compose?

Martin was a very good poet.

32. At age eight, whose works was I reading?

I was reading Shakespeare at that age. I was also proficient in Greek, Latin, German, Hebrew, French and English.

33. As I said earlier, why did I have a love/hate relationship with my hometown Vienna?

Vienna was largely Roman Catholic so there were anti-Semitic attitudes among the population. Also, Vienna was economically in decline. Vienna was also a very prudish culture, which, for someone like me whose teachings were strongly sexual made it difficult to work or win popularity.

34. When did I graduate from medical school?

First, I started medical school at age seventeen in 1873 and graduated in 1881. It took me longer than usual.

35. What was my first published work?

It was <u>On Aphasia</u>, in 1891, a condition in which a patient cannot pronounce or recognize words.

36. How would I describe myself?

Again, I was a bit of a loner. I was a control freak and an obsessive person, perhaps suffering from obsessive compulsive disorder as the nomenclature has it today. I was superstitious about numbers. Accuracy was important to me.

37. Did I have a heart attack?

Yes, in 1930, and supposedly it ended my cigar days.

38. Did I ever use hypnosis in my practice?

Yes, I did, but I found it ineffectual.

39. What did I think about the human mind?

I believe it was divided between that part of the mind that wanted to release emotions and that part of the mind that wanted to repress these emotions, thus creating resistance.

40. After medical school, I went into the medical research field and what project was I assigned?

I was assigned a project which required dissecting male eels to see if they had sex organs. I enjoyed the medical research field in medicine.

41. Why did I move out of the research field and into general practice?

Frankly, I needed the money. I had a wife and family to take care of now.

42. What two new ideas did I bring to the discipline of psychology?

First, I espoused that hysteria is not only a neurological concern but also a psychological one. Second, the unconscious part of the mind can affect behavior.

43. When did I first used the term "Psychoanalysis"?

I used it in 1896. It was a technique of "free association" where the client just speaks his mind, without hindrance. The patient is known as the analysand.

44. What two theories of mine did I come to abandon?

One was the seduction theory which said that the unconscious mind had repressed child abuse and thus brought on neurosis. However, seeing that a couple of my children had suffered neurosis, what would that say about me, their father? Also, there was the pressure technique in which the analyst would press on the forehead or temple area to overcome resistance. This also did not really work either.

45. So, what made this new "psychoanalysis" of mine work?

It put the patient in charge of the session. The analyst would be able to coach or probe as needed but the client for the most part would simply talk out loud. Childhood memories coming to the surface was a very important function of psychoanalysis.

46. What tragic event occurred in 1896 that brought me undo grief?

My father passed away. It was both a blessing and a curse this death of his.

47. Why in some ways was my father's death a blessing?

It motivated me to take a real solid analysis of myself and come to know myself better. It is during this approximately three year period from his death that I wrote my famous <u>The Interpretation of Dreams</u>.

48. So what two methods did I leave behind as a legacy for current psychoanalysis today?

Those two would be the free association method and dream analysis.

49. What was one of the earliest recorded treatments of neurosis using psychoanalysis?

It is the case of Dora, an 18 year old girl who Freud was not quite able to get satisfactorily treated.

50. What did dreams mean to me?

To me, all dreams are wish fulfillments. During sleep, the unconscious mind can let go so to speak. But, every dream strives for something.

51. Do I believe that dreams are generated from one's recent events or activities?

No, I do not. Well, when pressed, I can concede that not all dreams necessarily are born of infantile desires.

52. What do I mean by the "manifest" and latent contents of dreams?

It is the part of the dream that your mind actively remembers. The latent part of the dream is that part which comes out during psychoanalysis.

53. What term did I coin in 1895?

I used the word "transference". This was a process where the patient would begin to project emotions and feelings for someone else onto his or her therapist. This transference could be positive or negative.

54. What did my psychoanalysis prove to psychology?

It evidenced that psychoanalysis was not limited to abnormal psychology. It could be used to a wider audience.

55. How did I see two opposing human behaviors?

One I called the Pleasure Principle and the other I called the Reality Principle.

56. What is this Pleasure Principle of mine?

It is basically the seeking of pleasure but more so the avoidance of pain. It is what drives the id. I see that sexual urges mostly drive this behavior. I take a pessimistic view of the Pleasure Principle as not so much that it is joy seeking or recognizing beauty but that it avoids pain.

57. What is this Reality Principle of mine?

This is a sublimation of the libido to bring behavior into socially acceptable standards. It is the adult in us. If this libido is not channeled properly, I believe psychological damage can be done.

58. What is this you ask about something I called the "death drives"?

Basically, it speaks to mankind's aggressiveness or an individuals own aggression, misanthropy or bullying behavior. As opposed to Eros, love, it coexists with the death drive (Thanatos) and are not adversarial.

59. What are these things I call "parapraxes"?

They are my Freudian slips that everyone seems to have heard and are familiar as to the types.

60. What are parapraxes?

They include not remembering peoples' names, forgetting to do something unintentionally, loose lips, writing down the wrong thought, mishearing or misreading, losing things, not have accurate memory of events and bungling actions.

61. What did I think about jokes?

Again, repression and sublimation come into play. The unconscious mind is coming forward. I was fascinated by jokes so much that I wrote a book on it, <u>Jokes and Their Relation to the Unconscious</u>.

62. What two types of jokes did I state?

Tendentious jokes were locker room talk, aggressive, foul and sexually oriented types of jokes. Innocent jokes were puns and riddles. I came to believe that all jokes were tendentious as I saw innocent jokes as foreplay to tendentious humor.

63. What was one of my most controversial works?

That would be <u>Moses and Monotheism</u>. I wrote it in 1939 as one of my final publications. It struck a nerve as I denied that Moses was Hebrew but that he was Egyptian. It did not sit well with my Jewish community. I underwent a lot of pressure not to release it.

64. Do I believe that the Israelites killed Moses out of rebellion?

Yes, I do. Later, the Israelis would unify with another monotheistic religion. They also regretted killing Moses and then hoped for a Messiah, as Moses, would return. I say this is where Jewish guilt comes from.

65. Am I guilty of reading "sex" into much of my teachings?

I am guilty as charged. My contemporaries said that sexual energy did not arrive until puberty. I countered that by advocating that even infants had sexual energy.

66. How else did I break from traditional views on sexuality?

I saw the homosexual (known as invert behavior) as disliking the opposite sex. I saw perverts in those who had fetishes and the like. I also saw those who had experienced childhood sexual experiences.

67. When did I first meet Karl Abraham (1877-1925)?

I first met him in 1907. He was my best pupil and lifelong friend.
I outlived Karl.

68. When did I first meet Max Eitingon (1881-1943)?

I first met him in 1907 as well. Born in Russia, speculation abound that he may have served in the KGB.

69. When did I first meet Sandor Ferenczi (1873-1933)?

I first met him in 1908. He was chief neurologist at the Elizabeth Poorhouse in Budapest.

70. When did I first meet Ernest Jones (1879-1958)?

I first met him in April, 1908. He was the one person I trusted to do my biography, a three volume set.

71. When did I first meet Otto Rank (1884-1939)?

We first met in 1905. I was impressed with his encyclopedic reading abilities.

72. When did I first meet Hanns Sachs (1881-1947)?

I first formerly met Hanns at the Wednesday Psychology Society in 1909.

73. Who was one of my favorite English authors?

I enjoyed the writings of Rudyard Kipling.

74. What flower was I particularly fond of?

There was a flower, rare, to be found in Austria named Kohlroeserl (Nigritella nigra) a perfumy sweet dark purplish flower, almost black. They had sentimental value to me as, when my wife and I were newly married, I climbed up a ways to get her some of these rare flowers.

75. What was one of my favorite holiday places to visit?

It was the small peninsula of St. Bartholomae near the southerly end of the lake in Germany.

76. Why did I carry lemon juice in my pocket when visiting my favorite place, St. Bartholomae?

There was a glacier there with cold water and I would tell my children that lemon would add flavor. Lemon juice was just not a typical item to carry on one's person but I did.

77. Was Vienna still a male-dominated culture while I resided there?

Yes, in a sense, women were second class citizens with males still heads of households.

78. Did I like bicycles?

No, I did not nor did I like motorcycles. However, this did not stop me from buying them for my children.

79. How did I prepare my works?

I wrote everything in long hand using a quilted pen with the finest nibs available. I did not use a typewriter nor did I dictate any of my letters or other literary works.

80. How obsessed with timeliness was I?

I was never less than a half an hour early for any travel plans, for example, a train departure. I made sure that I would not miss my transportation.

81. In what book written by me in 1929 laid out my thoughts about civilization?

It was Civilization and its Discontents. In this, I theorize that civilization is a clash between the individual Pleasure principle and societal harmony. Ironically, individuals are most happy when operating under the Pleasure principle which is why I believe that people in general are unhappy in society due to pressures to conform. Man is basically aggressive and libidinous.

82. What is the first law of civilization?

That is justice. Without justice, there would be no laws. With no laws, there would be no civilization.

83. What were my thoughts on war?

I basically am a pacifist. I am confounded to see how man can commit such aggressions. It leads me to believe that man is intrinsically evil as well as good. People can, depending on the circumstances, do the wrong, or evil, action or take the high road. Again, to emphasize, humans have sexual urges constantly but rape cannot be tolerated and is an evil act.

84. What was my influence on the arts & literature?

I believed that all art eminated from libinous urges. I did influence the world of art by creating a style of writing called stream of consciousness.

85. In the previous book, I was asked about defense mechanisms, I reviewed two briefly. What are those two again and the remaining? What purpose do they serve?

They are reaction formation, regression, rationalism, fantasy, projection, displacement, denial and repression. They serve as a way (improper as it is) to deal with anxiety.

86. What is this thing I call repression?

It is when the unconscious mind does not permit certain experiences or trauma to see the light of day. Our memories could conceivably block out an entire experience with no hopes of recall.

87. What do I mean by denial?

Here, unlike repression which is not recalled, the event or trauma is known to the conscious mind but is not recognized, thus denied.

88. What is displacement?

Repressed feelings or emotions are bottled up and are released not at oneself but projected onto another. For example, a customer service representative has an angry client who did not pay his bill but the client takes his anger out at the representative, not himself.

89. What is projection?

Here the party parodies back that they are not the problem but someone else is, thus projecting the behavior to an innocent party.

90. What about fantasy?

Actually, some fantasy is very good and very healthy. It becomes pathological when one cannot decipher between fact and fiction.

91. What do I mean by rationalization?

It allows a person to push off blame to someone so they do not suffer a blow to their own ego. It permits one to alleviate guilt and shirk responsibility.

92. What is reaction formation?

Here an individual may exhibit negative behavior toward someone when, in fact, they like the person. One can think of young school age boys knocking over girls' lunch boxes. The boys most likely have a fondness for the girls.

93. How many letters did I write to my fiancee while we were away from each other for three years?

I wrote 900 letters in that time, I was very much in love.

94. When did I start my private practice?

I started right after I got married at age 30.

95. What special practice did I do before any lectures?

I would take a brisk half hour walk.

96. When did I get the first diagnosis of my jaw cancer?

I received the news in 1923. I had 33 subsequent operations.

97. Was I really offered $25,000 to psychoanalyze two American murderers?

Yes, I was but I turned it down.

98. Is it possible that I had an affair with my wife's sister, Minna?

I cannot kiss and tell but there does appear to be some evidence that Minna got pregnant and had an abortion.

99. Was I really an arrogant physician?

No, I don't think so. I ranged in my belief in myself from great confidence at times to self-doubt, even depression.

100. Was there any museums dedicated to me?

Yes, there are two current active museums dedicated to me. One "Sigmund Freud Museum" is at Berggasse 19, 1090 Vienna, Austria, http://www.freud-museum.at/en/.

101. Where is the other museum?

The other is located in the home where I passed away. It is Freud Museum London at 20 Maresfield Gardens, London, NW3, 5SX, https://www.freud.org.uk/.

Acknowledgements:

Sigmund Freud, shaper of the unconscious mind: Richard Stevens

Sigmund Freud, Man and Father: Martin Freud

The Secret Ring: Phyllis Grosskurth

Understanding Freud: Ruth Snowden

Wikipedia